THE
BISON
AND THE GREAT PLAINS

Text and photographs
Dave Taylor

Animals and their Ecosystems Series

Crabtree Publishing Company

A
Bobbie
Kalman
Book

Animals and Their Ecosystems Series
Dave Taylor

Editor-in-Chief
Bobbie Kalman

Editors
Christine Arthurs
Marni Hoogeveen
Janine Schaub

Design and pasteup
Adriana Longo

All photographs by Dave Taylor

For Ashley

I am especially grateful to my wife, Anne, and my brother-in-law, Jim Markou, who both accompanied me on the various trips required to photograph this book.

The majority of the pictures were taken in various national and state parks in North and South Dakota and Wyoming. I thank the park rangers and naturalists who assisted me in my quest to record a bit of history.

Cataloguing in Publication Data

Taylor, J. David, 1948-
    The bison and the Great Plains

(Animals and their ecosystems)
Includes index.
ISBN 0-86505-366-9 (bound) ISBN 0-86505-396-0 (pbk.)

1. Bison - Juvenile literature. 2. Bison - Ecology - Juvenile literature. 3. Ecology - Great Plains - Juvenile literature. I. Title. II. Series.

QL737.U5T3 1990   j599.73'58

350 Fifth Ave	1110 Kamato Road	73 Lime Walk
Suite 3308	Unit 4	Headington
New York	Mississauga, Ontario	Oxford 0X3 7AD
NY 10118	Canada L4W 2P3	United Kingdom

Contents

The bison and the Great Plains

The Great Plains of one hundred and fifty years ago was a vast, rolling grassland area with very few trees. This huge prairie covered about one third of North America. It stretched west to the Rocky Mountains and east to the Mississippi River and beyond. The northern border was formed by the dense forests in northern Canada. From there the Great Plains extended south, almost reaching the Gulf of Mexico.

Today a great many people live throughout this region. Cities, towns, and farmland cover much of the rolling plain. At one time, however, it was completely open and unsettled. Known as the wild west, it was the home of a multitude of plants and animals.

(left) In the 1800s the Great Plains stretched across the middle third of North America.

One animal, in particular, stood out against the background of the vast wilderness. At first glance it resembled a large brown bull with a big hump on its shoulders and a pair of thick, curved horns. It was covered with long, shaggy fur. Most people call it a buffalo, but its proper name is the American bison. At one time, millions of bison roamed freely on the Great Plains. This animal has since become a symbol of the Old West.

Let us travel back to the time of the bison and find out how Mandan, a cow bison, lived in her natural habitat. We have named Mandan after the Indian tribe that lived in her region. We will learn about the habits of North America's largest land mammal and meet the other animals that shared its ecosystem.

(above) The bison is a famous symbol of the Old West.

Mandan's herd

One fine spring day Mandan was grazing on a stretch of plain near what is now the Canadian border. Mandan is a member of a small herd that grazes in this area most of the year. Bison herds are composed of females called cows, their calves, and older offspring called yearlings. They lead a wandering lifestyle because of their eating habits. To support their large frames, bison spend most of their time feeding on vegetation such as wild oats and rye, wheat, lichen, speargrass, and various berries. They travel over large areas, called ranges, in constant search of food.

Bison gatherings

Some books and films give the false impression that the bison lived in vast groups numbering in the millions. The early settlers reported seeing herds that were so huge that it took the settlers several days to pass the animals. The settlers believed that the bison always traveled in such large groups. In fact, bison only gathered in these great numbers in autumn before migrating to their winter pastures. Twenty to fifty bison is the size of an average herd, and the largest herds of bison hold no more than two hundred animals. The size of a herd changes due to births and deaths and can be as small as just a few animals. This spring Mandan's herd consists of only twenty bison.

Who's the boss?

Bison society is based on strength. Within Mandan's herd the animals rank themselves from strongest to weakest. This method of ranking animals within a herd creates a dominance hierarchy because the stronger animals always dominate the weaker ones. The high-ranking cows earn their positions by winning shoving matches. Their rank gives them the authority to choose the herd's drinking or grazing spots but does not guarantee leadership. Other cows also lead the herd from time to time.

Mandan ranks near the top of the hierarchy in her herd. Because of her position, she can often make the other cows and yearlings move by just walking towards them.

A lone bull

Some distance away from the herd stands a lone male bison, called a bull. He has spent the winter in a forested area protected from the wind. There he fed on the dead grasses under the snow and managed to stay healthy and strong. He spent part of the time in the company of other bulls. Bull bison do not bond together in herds as the cows do. They remain independent because they are so immense that they do not need the protection that a herd provides. Some days this bull may be found in a group of several males, and other days he may be off on his own without another bison in sight.

Plain survival

Nearly twice the size of cows, bulls weigh between eighteen hundred and two thousand pounds (eight hundred kilograms and one tonne) and stand about seven feet (two meters) tall at the shoulder. Cows reach only four-and-a-half feet (one-and-a-third meters) in height. A bison lives about twenty years. Few predators dare to cross a strong, healthy bull. They prefer hunting the young or sick bison. Many bison die from accidents or severe winter conditions on the plains. Only the healthy animals survive. In this way, nature ensures that the animal population will be composed of only the strongest animals.

(opposite, top) Cow bison live in herds for both safety and companionship.

(opposite, bottom) This large cow bison is Mandan. She and the other cows in the herd rely on one another to spot danger.

8

Calving time

Mandan's herd does not wander very far today because some of the cows are almost ready to give birth. Animals that live in herds tend to have their calves within a few weeks of one another. This is nature's way of protecting the helpless newborn calves. Bison babies are easy prey on the plains where there are few places to hide, but because many calves are born in a short period of time, predators such as wolves and grizzly bears cannot possibly catch them all. Only half survive beyond the first month, but if their births were spread out over a longer period of time, even more would be eaten by predators.

Giving birth to a baby bull

Mandan leaves the herd, looking for a place to deliver her calf. Because there are no trees for protection, she settles for a shallow depression in the grass. She has carried the calf for nine-and-a-half months, and now it is time to bring a new life onto the plains. Mandan is in great danger when she gives birth because predators can easily attack her. Luckily she is the first in the herd to calve, so the wolves and bears are not yet on the lookout for newborns. Once the other cows start delivering, however, the predators will be close at hand, and many calves will be eaten.

Getting to know baby

Mandan lies on her side as soon as the birth process begins. After two hours of pushing and resting, she produces a wet, reddish brown blob. She rises to take a look at the damp mass at her feet and then nuzzles her nose into it. Mandan chews off the wet birth sac that still covers the baby. Inside is her first calf, a baby bull. As she licks her offspring clean, his smell becomes familiar to her. She will never forget it. This process is called imprinting. Imprinting enables a mother bison to recognize her baby by its scent, which is different from the smell of all the other calves on the plain. The calf also memorizes the scent of his mother.

Although he is helpless, the newborn bison is fully developed when he is born. His big, brown eyes open wide, and a fuzzy coat of rust-colored fur covers his body. The bison calf looks much like a barnyard calf but is a lot bigger.

(opposite) Mandan's calf is reddish-orange in color. As he gets older, his coat becomes dark brown.

(below) Mandan's calf learns to stand soon after he is born. As soon as he is able, he follows his mother wherever she goes.

The first feeding

Even before he is dry, the young male calf tries to stand up. He is hungry and wants to eat. His first attempts at standing land him smack on the ground, but hunger urges him to rise again. Within forty minutes the calf is on his feet, although his legs are still a little wobbly. Looking for food, he nuzzles his mother. His instincts tell him that she can provide him with nourishment.

Baby bison nurse by suckling on their mothers' teats. At first the baby calf does not know which part of Mandan gives the milk. He explores her lowered head but soon discovers that it is a waste of time. Next he tries her belly, but it produces no results either. Finally he locates the udder beneath her rear legs, where Mandan's milk is stored. He gives it a sharp butt with his head. This shoving action helps the milk start flowing.

Just as other mammals do, bison cows produce milk for their offspring. Calves nurse standing up.

Mandan—a mammal mother

Mandan is able to feed her young from her own body because she is a mammal. Female mammals have mammary glands that produce milk after the mothers have given birth. At first, baby mammals are unable to find or chew their own food, so they rely on their mother for nourishment. Mother's milk is the very best food that a mammal baby can have. The milk of each mammal species has nutrients that meet the particular needs of the babies of that species.

Mammal babies nurse in different ways. Some lie down beside their mothers when they nurse. Mandan's baby nurses standing up. He learns to stand and walk right away because he must move with the herd soon after he is born. Mandan's calf will drink his mother's milk until he is around seven months old. A week after his birth, however, he starts to nibble on grasses as well. As he eats more and more grass, he drinks less and less milk. The change from drinking milk to eating solid food is called weaning.

Easy prey

Even though she has just had a baby, Mandan is eager to get back to the herd. She knows that to stay alone could mean death for herself and, especially, her small calf. A lone cow and calf on the prairie are easy prey. A circling raven spots some bits of the birth sac, lands, and begins feeding on it. The circling of the raven is a signal to predators that food is nearby. To avoid being attacked, Mandan and her calf return to the herd as soon as possible.

Safe in the center

The firstborn calf attracts a lot of attention from the curious mothers-to-be, but the calf takes all the nuzzling in stride and stays close to his mother. The novelty soon wears off as more and more youngsters are born.

Young calves stay close to their mothers for about three weeks. After that, they start socializing with the other calves in the herd. They play tag and butt their heads against one another. Their play helps strengthen their muscles and gives them skills they will need later on. The adults guard the youngsters closely by keeping them enclosed in the center of the herd.

By the time the calves are eight weeks old, their humps and horns have started to grow. Slowly their coats turn dark brown to match the color of their mothers. At four years of age the calves are fully grown and ready to reproduce.

(above) Young calves stay close to their mothers for protection. Soon they will join the rest of the herd.

Bison facts

The bison's family tree

In order to better understand the world around us, scientists have divided plants and animals into special groups. Bison belong to the ox family. Other members of this family are the buffalo, goat, sheep, muskox, and yak. All these animals have hoofs, horns, and chew their cud. The ox family is a subgroup of a larger group that contains all the other hoofed animals such as the camel, moose, pig, and hippopotamus. All these in turn belong to the large order of animals commonly known as mammals.

That's no buffalo!

Although both the bison and buffalo belong to the ox family, there are some differences between them. The most noticeable difference is that buffalo horns are much longer and curve more than bison horns do. Buffalo do not have the bison's massive shoulders, nor do they have as much hair. A hidden difference between the two is that buffalo have thirteen pairs of ribs, whereas bison have fourteen pairs. Most bison live in North America, but buffalo live all over Africa and Asia.

The African buffalo live in herds.

Coming to America

The bison cannot claim to be a true North American species, one that first evolved on this continent. Its ancestors originally came from the large land mass that is now Europe and Asia. About one hundred thousand years ago the ancestors of Mandan crossed over a bridge of land that once stretched between Asia and North America.

Plains bison have smaller shoulder humps and weigh less than wood bison.

Ways of escape

At first glance bison do not look as if they need to worry too much about defending themselves. In fact, their fearsome size and sharp horns are enough to scare away most potential predators. Grizzly bears, packs of wolves, coyotes, and mountain lions, however, sometimes manage to kill bison. Bison have many special features that help them defend themselves out on the open plain. Their excellent senses of hearing and smell alert them to approaching danger. Unfortunately, their eyesight is poor. Sometimes their best chance is to flee quickly. Thin legs and large lungs help bison make fast getaways.

What are wood bison?

People often forget that there are two kinds of American bison—the plains bison and the lesser-known wood bison. Wood bison are larger, darker, and woolier than their close relatives. They tend to live in the wooded areas of Canada, the northern range of the plains bison. Like the plains bison, however, they have come very close to becoming extinct. At one time only a handful were left but, because of conservation efforts, around nine hundred wood bison now live in a few areas set aside especially for them.

Wood bison are bigger and darker than their cousins, the plains bison.

Special features

Compared with other horned animals, bison have rather short horns, and both male and female bison have them. Horns are used to establish rank in the herd. As members of the ox family, bison have hoofs. Their hoofs are cloven, or split down the middle. This feature makes it easier to climb rocky surfaces and walk on soft, muddy ground. Two-layered fur is a special feature that allows bison to cope with the extreme cold of prairie winters. The longer, outer layer of guard hair is thick and waterproof. Air gets trapped between the guard hair and underfur, creating a natural layer of insulation.

Massive munchers

Members of the ox family have curious eating habits. Like their relatives, bison always seem to be munching on something. Even when they are not grazing, their beards are moving up and down, a telltale sign that they are chewing. Because bison must graze out on the open prairie in plain view of predators, they prefer to eat as much as possible and chew later. After breaking off the grasses with their teeth, they swallow their food whole. Then they retire to a protected area where they can chew in peace. Here they bring back up the unchewed food, called cud, from their stomachs. They chew their cud thoroughly before swallowing it again. This method of feeding is called ruminating.

Animals that chew their cud have special multi-chambered stomachs that allow them to eat in this manner. The first chamber is a storage area filled with powerful agents that prepare the food for digestion. The animal retrieves its cud from this chamber. After the cud has been chewed, it passes by the first chamber and enters the next, where it is broken down further. Ruminating is an ideal adaptation to a diet of hard-to-digest grasses. This long process of digestion also allows the bison to absorb more vitamins from their food.

Bison ruminate, or chew their cud, when they feel safe.

Where the bison roamed

The Great Plains of one hundred and fifty years ago were rich and varied. This grassland area formed a wide band of open wilderness through the center of the continent. Because it was far away from large bodies of water, the heartland of North America received only a limited amount of rainfall.

There were two distinct areas on the Great Plains. Both east and west were often referred to as prairies, but only the east was a true long-grass prairie. In general, more rain fell on the eastern plain, so the vegetation was lush. The grass grew as tall as an average person! Farther west were the plains, where the land was higher and much drier, resulting in shorter grass.

Hills and forests

The grassland was not the only habitat on the Great Plains. Between the prairies and the plains were several small ranges of hills. The hills received more rainfall because they forced the clouds higher, causing them to cool and lose their moisture. As a result, the hills and surrounding areas were covered in forests.

Mandan lived near the Black Hills, given this name because the dark tree trunks made the hills look black from a distance.

The Rockies

At the western edge, the plains merged with the forested slopes of the Rocky Mountains. The change in the landscape was gradual where the forest and the plain merged in the foothills. In other places the lush mountains appeared to soar straight up from the grass. Here the land received plenty of moisture, allowing dense forests to grow.

The badlands

The Great Plains also contained some desert areas. These deserts were found in deep valleys, which were formed by glaciers many centuries ago. Fast-flowing rivers, heavy rains, and fierce winds also played a part in fashioning the unusual landscape of the badlands. Strange pillars of rock and steep cliffs scarred the face of this barren land. The region became known as the badlands because it was extremely hazardous to cross.

On the move

Bison herds wandered through all these different habitats, but some parts were more suitable for grazing than others. In the east, an area of a certain size grew enough grass to feed about thirty bison for a year. In the west, where there were scrubbier types of grass, an area of equal size could feed only one bison. To survive, these huge animals were constantly on the move, leaving behind vast tracts of land where the vegetation had been chewed to the ground. By the time the bison returned, the grasses would have grown back.

Dry times

On the Great Plains winters were very cold, and summer temperatures were scorching. Grass was the most abundant form of vegetation because it could withstand the extreme conditions. Long periods without rain, called droughts, occurred from time to time. The grass plants were able to stay alive because they have large, efficient root systems. The bison survived droughts by traveling long distances to water holes. Somehow they remembered where to find these places, even when several years passed between droughts.

(below) In spring, water holes dot the plains.

Water supplies

Several major rivers crossed the Great Plains, and small bodies of water were also scattered here and there. In the northeastern part of the range millions of tiny ponds were created each spring when the prairie snows melted into water, which made its way into the small depressions on the plains. These ponds evaporated by the end of summer.

(opposite) On the long-grass prairie, bison did not have to compete for food.

(below) Trees grew abundantly only on the hills.

The prairie ecosystem

Mandan lives on the huge eastern prairie, where there is an abundance of long grasses. The non-living environment, which includes the soil, water, energy, and gases in the air, provides a solid basis for a stable and varied ecosystem. An ecosystem is a community of plants and animals in a particular area that depend on one another for survival. On the prairie the grass is the foundation of the ecosystem because it is the main producer. As a producer, grass is able to take in energy from the sun and transform it into food energy for the animals that eat it.

Passing on food energy

Animals and insects are unable to make their own energy. They are called consumers because they must get their food energy either directly or indirectly from plants. Plant-eating animals, known as herbivores, receive their food energy directly from plants. Carnivores, or meat-eating animals, get their food energy indirectly. They eat herbivores or other animals that eat herbivores, which in turn get their food energy from plants. The way in which energy is passed along in an ecosystem is called a food chain. Many food chains form a food web.

Badgers eat many of the small animals found on the plains, including prairie dogs.

An interconnected community

All sorts of grazers and browsers live on the vegetation of the prairie. Grazers eat grass, so they live on the open grassland. Large grazers such as bison and elk must graze big areas in order to satisfy their food needs. Browsers, such as deer, rely on shrubs and leaves, so they tend to live in wooded areas. Grasshoppers and other plant-eating insects are very important to the prairie ecosystem. They are eaten by many small animals and birds, which are then eaten by carnivores. Other small animals such as prairie dogs, squirrels, and mice, which feed on grass, seeds, and roots, are also food for carnivores.

Carnivores obtain their food in a variety of ways. Predators get their food by hunting and killing other animals or insects. On the other hand, scavengers such as ravens do not hunt. They eat the leftovers of predators. The grizzly bear preys on the bison, but it also eats berries and leaves. Animals that have mixed diets are called omnivores.

Predators play an important role in the prairie ecosystem because they keep the population of smaller animals under control. The waste material produced by all the animals returns nutrients to the soil to help the grasses grow. Certain insects and fungi, called decomposers, help break down these materials into nutrients so that they can be reused by plants. Nothing is wasted in an ecosystem that is left in its natural state.

Bird populations

Many parts of the Great Plains provide ideal conditions for large bird populations. The springtime ponds are excellent habitats for nesting birds and ducks. By the time the water dries up, the young goslings and ducklings are ready to fly to staging areas. Millions of birds gather at staging areas to feed and rest before heading south for the winter.

Along the riverbanks Mandan's herd encounters the largest birds of the plains—trumpeter swans and white pelicans. A variety of blackbirds, songbirds, herons, and cranes can also be found along the forested edges of the rivers. The passing bison help provide them with food. As the herds graze, they stir up insects on which many of these birds feed. The birds stay close to the bison, waiting to catch the insects that fly up.

(right) In spring white pelicans fly in to fish in the prairie rivers. These pelicans do not dive for fish as brown pelicans do. Instead they cruise up and down the river, alone or in groups, scooping up fish near the surface of the water.

(below) Trumpeter swans make their nests along rivers. The largest of North America's swans, these birds can be spotted leading their broods of cygnets to choice feeding grounds.

Grazers and browsers

The bison shared the Great Plains with a variety of plant eaters. Some were grazers; others were browsers. The pronghorn antelope ranged on the western part of the plains. Being a browser, it preferred to munch on the sagebrush that grew on the short-grass plain. At one time the pronghorn was as numerous as the bison.

Prairie elk and deer

The elk, a large species of deer, preferred a habitat in which both grass and trees could be found. It fed on the grass during the cool of the night and retreated to the shade of the riverside woods during the day. Some people mistakenly believe that the elk is a mountain animal. At one time elk roamed throughout the Great

Plains. Unfortunately, the prairie elk was hunted until it became extinct. The only elk that survived were those protected by the mountain forests.

Mule deer and white-tailed deer lived in the forest valleys of the Great Plains. These browsers fed on the leaves and twigs of trees rather than on grass. They seldom ventured onto the open plains, preferring instead the food and shelter of the treelined rivers.

(above) Elk were once very common on the prairie, but overhunting eliminated most of them. The remaining herds were forced into the mountainous forest regions, where they can be found today.

(above) Unlike elk, which shed their antlers every year, bighorn sheep keep their horns for life.

Bighorn sheep

Surprisingly enough, a few animals were able to live in the barren badlands. One of these was the bighorn sheep. Bighorn sheep were a common sight in the safety of the steep cliffs, but they spent half their time in greener pastures, especially meadows. Bighorn sheep have massive spiral horns. During mating season, males fight in spectacular head-cracking duels .

(right) The pronghorn antelope is not really an antelope. It is the only surviving member of an ancient family of animals that originated in North America. This makes the pronghorn antelope a true North American species.

A prairie-dog town

Prairie dogs also made their home on the Great Plains. During the time that the bison roamed freely, prairie dogs formed a rich wildlife community. These ground squirrels lived in towns made up of interconnecting tunnels and burrows. The total number of prairie dogs living on the plains during Mandan's time is unknown, but some people claim there were over five billion.

Underground neighborhoods

A prairie-dog town is like a city made up of several neighborhoods. Each neighborhood has boundaries within which related females and their offspring live. A single male also lives in each neighborhood and chases other males away. The females do not allow unrelated females in their area either, although young prairie dogs are allowed to wander wherever they wish. Prairie-dog family groups are very close. The animals often sleep together, and there is always much hugging and sniffing.

Dig this!

Prairie dogs have front paws with extra-long claws to help them dig tunnels. They loosen the soil with their sharp claws, pass the dirt under their bodies, and then kick it out with their hind feet. The tunnels go down about ten feet (three meters) and may extend fifty feet (fifteen meters) from one entrance to another. They are quite warm inside because of their under-ground location. The many rooms are lined with dried grasses.

Food for many

The prairie dog gets its name from the sound it makes when it is in danger. A guard dog usually keeps watch by standing up on the mound outside the tunnel. When he suspects trouble, he lets out a yelp to warn the others to scoot into their holes. Then he pops up a few moments later to see what is causing the commotion. If it is bison passing by, the prairie dogs get on with their business because the bison leave them alone. Not all the animals of the plains, however, ignore these little creatures. A prairie-dog town is a magnet for predators. Badgers, ferrets, hawks, coyotes, bobcats, and snakes all hunt the chubby squirrels. These small rodents reproduce frequently to keep up with the large numbers they lose to predators.

Enriching the ecosystem

Although greatly reduced in numbers, prairie dogs are still plentiful in the west. Besides being a valuable food source, they are essential to their ecosystem in other ways. They eat grass and small insects. Their droppings and constant digging enrich the soil, which in turn helps nourish the grass on which all the plains animals depend.

(above) When a prairie-dog tunnel is abandoned, other animals, such as these burrowing owls, inhabit it.

(opposite, top) Prairie dogs are rodents. Rodents are mammals that have large front teeth, which they use for gnawing.

(opposite, bottom) Ground squirrels are also rodents. Rodents are important in the prairie food web because they are eaten by many other animals.

Preying on the bison

Although the bison were strong and fearsome, they too were hounded by predators. Only a few species could hope to capture these huge beasts. The bison were threatened by the wolf, the coyote, the mountain lion, and the grizzly bear.

The buffalo wolf

One of the most numerous predators on the plains was the buffalo wolf. This animal was large, about the same size as the arctic wolf, which hunted the caribou. Some buffalo wolves weighed more than one hundred and fifty pounds (seventy kilograms). Most of them were white, but some were various shades of gray and black. Although these wolves were large, they were too small to attack an adult bison on their own. Like other wolves they lived in packs and seldom hunted alone. Hunting in numbers allowed them to tackle prey that was much larger than they were. As a general rule, the bigger the prey, the bigger the pack—and there was no bigger prey on the plains than the bison. Buffalo-wolf packs were among the largest ever seen, usually around twenty to thirty wolves. Sometimes packs of over fifty animals traveled together.

(above) Large wolves, usually whitish in color, once followed the herds of bison. The pioneers called them buffalo wolves.

Standing ground

Most of the time adult bull bison were more than a match for even the large wolf packs. The wolves would test a bull for signs of weakness and, if none were found, they would move on. An animal that stood its ground was much less likely to be attacked than one that ran. A bison that ran allowed the wolves to get close enough to take large bites out of its flanks and belly. The wolves would continue to disturb the wounded bison, so it could not rest or heal. About a day or two later the exhausted bison would finally collapse. The rich bounty of meat a bison would provide was worth the wait.

Banding together

Bison herds had a special method of defending themselves. One day a pack of wolves appeared before Mandan's herd. The cows instantly banded together and formed a solid wall of alert animals. All at once the wolves charged at the herd, hoping the frightened animals would start a stampede. If the cows scrambled and ran, the wolves would have been able to take several calves and possibly a cow or two as well. Mandan and the rest of the cows remained in position, however, and the wolves gave up and moved on. This time Mandan and her calf were safe.

Grizzlies of the plains

The grizzly bears of the plains were also much larger than their mountain relatives. These light-colored bears were capable of killing adult bison, but they usually preferred taking newborn calves. In spring the bears feasted on the bison and elk that died during the harsh winter. These carcasses provided a much-needed source of protein for the bears after their long winter sleep, called hibernation. Later in the year grizzlies killed bison that were sick or unfortunate enough to wander away from their herd while looking for food.

Grizzly bears rarely hunted healthy bison.

The breeding season

This bull does not let his mate out of sight.

As he wanders with the herd, Mandan's calf becomes acquainted with the other animals of the plains, but he has not yet seen a fully grown bison bull. One summer's day he finally comes face to face with the largest bison he has ever seen.

One big bull!

Mandan's calf hears a magnificent roar from the top of a nearby hill and turns in the direction of the sound. He sees what is obviously another bison, yet the bull is much bigger than any of the females. Something this big is scary enough for a young bison, but the bull's roaring is even more frightening. The male roars to announce that he is searching for a female. As the bull enters the herd, the calf hides behind Mandan. The bull is visiting the herd to see if any of the cows are ready to mate. As it is still too early for breeding, the bull wanders off again.

The rut

By midsummer the rut is in full swing. The term "rut" is a word scientists use to refer to the time of year when male elk, deer, moose, and bison are ready to breed. During mating season all the males of these species make "rutting," or roaring sounds. The bison bulls enter the rut before the cows are ready to mate, so they must wait a few weeks before breeding can take place.

When the lone bull returns to the herd a few weeks later, several females are ready to mate. This time, however, the bull has competition. Several other bulls have already arrived looking for mates. They each chose a female and started following her around. This courting behavior is called tending. Tending bulls take no notice of the new calves that are with their mothers. Older bull calves, though, are another matter. The mating bulls chase the yearlings away whenever they come too close to their mothers because they are considered competition.

Bellowing mating calls

The lone bull approaches the herd slowly and cautiously. He stops, watches for a minute, and then moves closer until, finally, he is within the limits of the herd. He bellows a long, gruntlike roar that rolls across the plains. The bull wishes to mate, but all the females are already taken. The bull senses, however, that he has a chance to chase one of the tending bulls away.

Sizing up the competition

During the breeding season bulls spend much of their time competing with one another. The size of the bull, the length of his horns, and the energy with which he performs his challenges all give clues to his strength. When two bulls come face to face, the weaker bull quickly recognizes that he can be beaten and looks away, signaling that he is giving up. These meetings help limit the number of injuries. All-out fights are rare, but sometimes bulls are injured and killed in battle. Only the strongest bulls have the chance to breed, ensuring that the new calves will also be strong. The result is a healthy herd.

Bulls show off by 1) bellowing, 2) urinating on the dust and pawing at it, and 3) rolling on the ground. 4) This sometimes leads to violent fights.

A show of power

A tending bull and his new rival face each other. To demonstrate his strength, the rival bull goes through a set of actions. He urinates on a prairie-dog mound or a patch of earth that he has scraped clean. Sometimes he rolls in the dirt, slamming his hump into the ground until he is surrounded by a halo of dirt. This is called wallowing. It is clear that the rival intends to fight for a female.

The two bulls stare at each other and bellow. Neither blinks nor backs down. They paw the earth and snort. Then they charge and ram heads. The long black hair on their heads cushions the blow, and their heavily coated shoulders take the racking of each other's horns. The tending bull slips and turns, giving the rival the opportunity to pierce him in the neck with his horn. Wounded, the loser flees, leaving the new bull to mate with the cow.

Bulls breed with as many cows as possible before they lose to another challenger. The cows, though, are not very cooperative about mating. Given the slightest chance, they bolt back into the center of the herd with the bulls chasing behind them.

The end of summer

As summer comes to a close, Mandan and the other bison become aware of the change in the weather. Their once rust-colored calves now have thicker, darker coats, and the adults are heavier and have more hair. Fewer and fewer bulls remain in this area of the plains. Most of the cows are pregnant, and the males are drifting off on their own. They will not meet up with Mandan's herd again until next summer.

The coming of winter

Winter on the Great Plains is a trying time for all animals, large and small. Prairie dogs escape the freezing cold by staying in their burrows where the temperature remains constant all year round. Others go into hibernation until

spring awakens them. The majority of birds migrate south, and some mammals travel long distances to places that offer greater protection from the winter winds and blizzards.

For the winter months bison migrate to the parts of their range that provide shelter, such as valleys and wooded areas. Several thousand cow herds, Mandan's included, join together for this massive movement. Their journey covers about two hundred miles (three hundred and twenty kilometers). When the pioneers first saw these huge gatherings, they mistakenly believed that bison herds were always this large.

(above) To get at the grass below, Mandan and other bison sweep their heads back and forth in the snow.

In winter and spring the bison in Mandan's herd must risk their lives by crossing icy and flooded rivers.

Mandan's herd has good reason to seek shelter. Even with their heavy coats, the bison find the roaring wind that sweeps down from the mountains to be a deadly foe. The herd copes with this inclement weather by huddling together for warmth and by facing headfirst into the wind. The two-layered fur of the bison is specially adapted to this weather.

Coping with snow

In winter bison manage to find food even though it is buried beneath layers of snow. The bison's wide nose acts as a built-in snow shovel. By sweeping its massive head and beard back and forth, the bison opens up a hole in the snow called a feeding crater. Even though these massive animals are well adapted to their freezing environment, winter always takes its

toll. Some bulls start winter in a tired and weak condition, and wolves find them easy prey. Calves, because of their smaller sizes, are more likely to feel the cold. They often fail to make it through the winter.

Treacherous river crossings

Crossing rivers is a major threat to the bison on their journeys. Each year many bison fall through the ice into the dangerous waters. Calves and weaker adults are the most likely to drown as the panicked animals try to reach the safety of the shore. These river crossings often leave the riverbanks littered with frozen dead animals, which are eagerly devoured by grizzlies and wolves in the spring. Mandan and her calf are fortunate enough to survive the winter.

Hunting the bison

For centuries the American bison thrived on the Great Plains. They were well adapted to their habitat and had few enemies. Because the predators usually killed off the young, sick, and weak animals, the herds stayed strong and healthy. If the bison population had not been kept in check, they would have destroyed their food supply by overgrazing. In this way, the balance of nature remained undisturbed.

The Plains Indians

The bison were hunted in limited numbers by the Plains Indians. The Plains Indians were tribes of native North American people who shared the Great Plains with the bison for thousands of years. These nomadic people followed the bison throughout its range. They lived in tents and went on hunting expeditions that lasted several months.

To the Indians, the bison meant staying alive. Besides eating their meat, the native people dried the bison's hide and used it to make clothing and tents. In spring the women collected the wooly hair the bison left behind on the plains and spun it into rope. In summer they picked up the droppings, which they used as fuel for their fires. The dung burned well because it consisted mostly of grass. Bison bones were fashioned into tools and weapons.

The great hunt

Hunting the bison was a great challenge. For the most part the Plains Indians only killed the number of bison they needed, so they never posed a threat to the herds. Sometimes they hunted small groups of bison with spears or drove them over cliffs in great numbers. The Indians would startle a group of animals, thereby causing them to break into a stampede. When horses arrived on the plains, hunting methods changed drastically. Tribes of Indians riding trained horses were able to follow the animals wherever they went.

The power of the gun

The traditional way of life in North America began to change in the 1800s when the first fur trappers, who hunted with guns, ventured onto the Great Plains. The early rifle could fire only one shot and then had to be reloaded. As time went on more powerful rifles, which could fire several shots quickly, were used. These weapons were a great threat to the bison because a whole herd could be killed off very quickly. All of a sudden the bison were at a huge disadvantage.

Transforming the plains

The first pioneers that traveled across the Great Plains on their way to the west coast had little interest in staying on the prairies. They found that they could not farm the grasslands, and their cattle could not survive its harsh winters. As time went on, however, more and more people came to live on the plains.

After the railroad was built, the settlers began farming the land that used to belong to the bison. Professional hunters killed the bison in great numbers to feed the men working on the railroad and to clear the way for farming. The wide-open plains were transformed into farms and villages. Soon the settlers and Indians began fighting with one another. Because the bison were so important to the Indians, the settlers decided to kill these animals. Once the Indians were deprived of their livelihood, their numbers dwindled.

The great slaughter

In 1860 over fifty million bison roamed the Great Plains. Within twenty years, the bison were all but wiped out. By 1889 only eighty-five free-roaming bison could be found in the entire United States! Another two hundred lived in Yellowstone National Park, and 550 were counted in Canada. There were 256 in zoos and private collections, for a total of 991 animals.

The slaughter on the plains continued until the 1920s. The bison was not the only animal to suffer tremendous losses. Both the grizzly bear and wolf almost disappeared. Bighorn sheep were an easy target for hunters. By the early 1900s not a single one was left on the plains. The prairie elk was hunted to extinction. The population of the pronghorn antelope, which once equalled the bison's numbers, was reduced drastically. Although a few pronghorn survived into the next century, their days on the wide-open plains were finished.

Descendants of horses brought to the New World by Spanish settlers made hunting bison much easier.

The bison's fate

And what happened to Mandan and her calf? Perhaps Mandan's grandchildren were among the remaining 991 animals left in 1889. Fortunately, there is a happy ending to the tragic story of the great slaughter on the plains. In recent years the American bison, which was once listed as an endangered species, has been brought back from the verge of extinction.

Saving the bison

In the early twentieth century the governments of Canada and the United States set up national parks where the bison were protected, and hunting bison became illegal. Rangers and people concerned about wildlife conservation took special care of the few remaining animals and nursed the herds back to health. Thanks to their efforts over thirty-five thousand bison now live in North America.

National parks play an important role in saving many species. These tracts of land are set aside for the purpose of preserving wildlife. The animals live as they would in the wild, but there are boundaries. Within the parks the animals are protected from hunters.

A valuable lesson

Huge herds of bison may never again roam the Great Plains as they did in Mandan's time, but Canadians and Americans have learned a valuable lesson. Because the bison were once so numerous, people thought there would always be plenty of animals to spare no matter how many were killed. This mistaken belief caused the near extinction of North America's largest land animal. From this close call we have learned that wildlife can be quickly destroyed if people do not treat it with care and respect.

The happy ending shows that many people do care about wildlife. They appreciate it and want to conserve it for future generations. You and I can visit the bison in national parks, watch them graze on the grasslands, look after their calves, and roll on prairie-dog mounds. Perhaps as we watch, we can drift back in time and picture Mandan and her calf roaming peacefully on the Great Plains.

(opposite) Wild herds of bison can still be found in places such as Yellowstone National Park, Wyoming.
Mandan grazes peacefully with her calf at her side.

Glossary

bellow - A long, gruntlike roar a bull makes during mating season to impress rivals and potential mates

browser - An animal that feeds on the leaves and shoots of bushes and trees

carnivore - A meat-eating animal

conservation - The act of protecting our natural resources, including animals, from being destroyed

cud - Partially digested food that must be chewed before full digestion can take place

decomposer - An organism such as a worm, fungus, or bacteria that reduces what it eats into nutrients, which are then returned to the environment

dominance hierarchy - The order, from strongest to weakest, in which some animals rank one another

drought - A prolonged period of dry weather; a lack of rain that causes the death of vegetation

ecosystem - The interdependent community of plants and animals and the surroundings in which they live

endangered - Close to becoming extinct

environment - The surroundings in which an animal or plant lives

extinct - Describing species that no longer exist

grazer - An animal that feeds on grass

habitat - The area in which a plant or animal naturally lives

herbivore - A plant-eating animal

herd - A group of wild animals that wanders together. Bison herds have between twenty and fifty members.

imprinting - The process by which a baby animal and its mother recognize each other

instinct - A natural drive to act in a certain way

lichen - A non-flowering plant that grows close to the ground and is found in northern regions

mammal - An animal that is warm-blooded, covered in hair, and has a backbone. A female mammal has mammary glands in which milk is produced.

mating - The breeding of a male and female of a species

migrate - To travel from one area to another during certain seasons or following the availability of food

nutrient - A substance that a living thing consumes to be healthy and strong

omnivore - An animal that eats both plants and animals

prairie - A long-grass plain

predator - An animal that hunts and kills other animals for food

range - The area of land where a species lives

rodent - A small mammal that has large front teeth, which it uses for gnawing

ruminating - A method of feeding that involves bringing cud back into the mouth to be chewed

rut - The period of time when certain male mammals make roaring noises because they are ready to mate

scavenger - An animal that feeds on the remains of animals that it did not hunt and kill

species - A distinct animal or plant group that shares similar characteristics and can produce offspring within its group

weaning - The process of changing the diet of a young mammal from milk to solid food

yearling - A one-year-old baby animal

Index

123456789 WP Printed in the U.S.A. 9876543210